Pain Raised Me: But Trauma Healed Me

Michaelia Nobles

Published by Stephanie M Seaton Author Publishing, 2024.

PAIN RAISED ME: BUT TRAUMA HEALED ME

First edition. October 8, 2024.

Copyright © 2024 Michaelia Nobles.

ISBN: 979-8227489197

Written by Michaelia Nobles.

Table of Contents

Pain Raised Me: Trauma Healed Me
by Michaelia Nobles

Synopsis

"Pain Raised Me but Trauma Healed Me" by Michaelia Nobles is a powerful and deeply personal narrative designed to inspire and encourage women who have faced or are currently enduring abuse. In this book, Michaelia reminds readers that no matter what challenges they face, God is always in control and can guide them through their darkest moments. Through her story, she emphasizes that true change begins within and that women should not allow their past to define or shape them. Instead, they should allow God to transform them into the women He is calling them to be. Drawing a poignant comparison to the biblical story of the woman with the issue of blood who pressed her way to touch Jesus after 12 long years, Michaelia's story is a testament to the power of faith, resilience, and healing. "Pain Raised Me but Trauma Healed Me" seeks to inspire every woman to break generational curses, step out of the shadows, and walk in victory and freedom over their past.

Introduction

In "Pain Raised Me but Trauma Healed Me," I, Michaelia Nobles, share my journey of pain, struggle, and ultimately, healing. This book is written for every woman who has faced abuse, felt broken, or questioned her worth. I know what it is like to be trapped in the darkness, to wonder if there is any hope left. But I also know the power of God's love and the transformation that comes when we allow Him to heal our deepest wounds.

This book is more than just my story; it is a guide for any woman seeking to break free from the chains of her past. By sharing my experiences and drawing on the powerful example of the biblical woman with the issue of blood, I aim to show that no matter how long you have suffered, there is always a way to reach out and touch the healing power of Jesus. My prayer is that as you read these pages, you will find the strength to break generational curses, step out of the shadows, and walk boldly into the future God has prepared for you.

Preface

"Pain Raised Me but Trauma Healed Me" was born out of a desire to bring hope and healing to women who have endured the unthinkable. For too long, I allowed the pain of my past to define me, to dictate my worth and my future. But God had other plans. He used the trauma I experienced to mold and shape me into the woman I am today, and now, I am compelled to share that journey with you.

The story I tell in this book is deeply personal, but it is also universal. Every woman who has ever faced abuse, who has ever felt the weight of generational curses, who has ever been tempted to live in the shadows, will find something in these pages that resonates with her own experience. My hope is that this book will serve as a beacon of light, guiding you through your darkest moments and reminding you that you are not alone.

I invite you to join me on this journey of healing and transformation. Together, we will walk the path that leads from pain to victory, from bondage to freedom, and from darkness to the radiant light of God's love.

Dedication

First, I give all glory and honor to God who is ahead of my life. I thank God for saving me and setting me free. If it were not for Him, I would not have made it to share this story with you.

To my beloved mother,

whose unwavering love and strength have been my guiding light, shaping me into the person I am today. Your endless sacrifices, patience, and resilience have taught me the meaning of true courage. Through every trial and triumph, you stood by me, always believing in me, even when I struggled to believe in myself. Your faith in me never wavered, and your encouragement was my source of strength when I felt weak. I am forever grateful for your wisdom, your prayers, and your unconditional love. Thank you for being my anchor, my confidante, and my greatest supporter.

To my siblings,

for the laughter, the support, and the countless shared memories that have shaped who I am. Your presence in my life is a gift that words can scarcely capture, but I hope this book serves as a small token of my appreciation. Thank you for being my constant source of inspiration and strength.

To my aunts—for being not only a constant source of wisdom, encouragement, and grace but also the shining examples of strength that I needed. You have each contributed to the foundation of my character, reminding me through your actions and your love that I am never alone. Your unwavering support has carried me through moments when I felt I could not go on, and for that, I am eternally grateful. I am blessed to have you in my life, and I carry your lessons in my heart always.

To my uncle dad—for stepping into my life with unconditional love and guidance, showing me what true family means. You have been a pillar of strength and compassion, offering not only advice but also a steady hand and a loving heart. You have shown me that family is not just defined by blood but by the love we share and the support we give. Your presence in my life has made all the difference, and I am forever thankful for your influence and care.

To my Bishop and First Lady—for your tireless spiritual leadership and for being true beacons of faith, hope, and inspiration. In times of confusion and doubt, your prayers, your wisdom, and your unwavering belief in God's plan for me provided the light that guided me through my darkest days. Your dedication to the ministry and to those you shepherds have left an indelible mark on my soul, and I am honored to walk in faith under your guidance.

To everyone who has supported me on this journey, whether with kind words, prayers, or acts of love, you have been a part of this story. This book is not only a testament to my journey but a reflection of the strength that comes from community and the profound power of faith. Your encouragement lifted me when I needed it most, and I could not have reached this point without you. Every word written, every lesson learned, is intertwined with the support you have shown me. For that, I am deeply, deeply thankful.

Chapter 1: Raised by Pain: The Shattered Dream

Psalm 34:18 - "The Lord is close to the brokenhearted and saves those who are crushed in spirit."

The Force of Pain

Pain is an unknowable force that both defines and challenges our existence. It is the uninvited guest at life's banquet, a relentless companion on our journey, a shadow that whispers and demands our attention. From the searing sting of physical injury to the profound ache of emotional wounds, pain unites us all in its grasp. But within its uncomfortable hold lies an inconsistent power transformative energy that can push us to our limits, revealing strengths we never knew we had. In pain's crucible, we find not just suffering but seeds of resilience, growth, and a deeper understanding of our humanity.

My introduction to this profound reality came at an early age, even before I fully understood it. Pain became a formidable force, shaping me into someone I did not recognize. The early memories of my life felt like a picture-perfect dream: mom, dad, my older brother, and me, the youngest. It was a dream I never wanted to come from, a world where I had everything for which I could wish. But this dream began to crumble.

The First Wound – My Father's Betrayal

At the age of six, I encountered my first experience with pain when my father revealed he had another daughter, whom he seemed to love more than me. I was too young to understand manipulation or emotional neglect. All I knew was that the man I adored, my father, no longer loved me the way I needed him to. The realization was overwhelming, he prioritized someone else over me.

This feeling of rejection gnawed at my self-esteem, making me feel invisible and inadequate. I was too young to understand why, and the unanswerable question haunted me: "Why wasn't I enough?" My world, which had been so bright, suddenly turned dark, and everything fell upside down. Despite the growing distance between us, my love for him remained, but it was now mixed with a sense of confusion and deep hurt.

The Fall of My Hero Alcohol and Aggression

As the years went by, my father's absence became more noticeable, even though he still lived with us. He slowly drifted away, and his choices, especially his growing dependency on alcohol, began to tear our family apart. The man who had once been my knight in shining armor became a dragon, breathing fire and destruction into every corner of our lives. His love for alcohol surpassed his love for us, and his presence in our lives faded with every passing day.

Witnessing my father's descent hurt me deeply, and my brother Tommy tried to shield me from the worst of it. But the conflict between my parents was impossible to ignore. The man who once cheered me on now grew hostile toward my mother. I could not understand why the person I had looked up to all my life was acting this way. Seeing my mother suffering under his aggression was unbearable, and it created an emotional divide in me.

It felt like I was being forced to choose between my parents, though neither of them ever asked me to. The pressure weighed on me, and I felt as if my world was being torn apart.

The Abandonment – Stranded at School

By the time I was eight, the cracks in my father's relationship with me had widened into a rift. One afternoon, I was left stranded at school, waiting for my father to pick me up. As the minutes turned into hours, my anxiety grew. My brother Tommy came to my rescue, but the fear that something terrible might happen overwhelmed me. As we waited at a nearby gas station, I saw my father's car drive up and down the street, looking for me.

In that moment, I asked myself: What could be more important than me? Why wasn't I, his priority? The unanswered questions continued to pile up as I spent the night with my grandma Rosie. She, too, tried to shield me from the harsh reality of the situation, but I could not help feeling abandoned and unwanted.

The Emotional Toll Alone in a Room Full of Love

This abandonment and neglect took a heavy toll on me emotionally and mentally. Frustration turned to anger as no one seemed willing to answer my questions or acknowledge my feelings. Even though I was surrounded by a loving support system of my brother, my mother, and my grandmother, I felt utterly alone. The sense of isolation was suffocating, and I convinced myself that no one really cared. My world, once filled with love and stability, had crumbled, leaving me to navigate the pieces on my own.

The Seeds of Resilience

As I look back on these moments, I realize that the pain I experienced in my childhood planted the seeds of resilience within me. My relationship with my father, once so full of admiration and love, became the source of my greatest pain. But it was through these struggles that I began to understand the need for change that had to start within me. Although I did not fully comprehend it at the time, God was guiding me through this journey, laying the foundation for the healing that would eventually come.

In this chapter, I reflect on how pain, though deeply uncomfortable, set the stage for growth, self-awareness, and eventually, healing. While the journey was far from over, it was in these early years that the battle with my pain began, shaping the woman I would become.

Chapter 2: Wounds Unseen: The Hidden Impact of Trauma

Psalm 147:3 - "He heals the brokenhearted and binds up their wounds." This verse speaks to the idea of hidden wounds and the healing that God provides for those who are brokenhearted.

Revenge as an Outlet

The anger I bottled up began manifesting in dangerous ways. Revenge became my coping mechanism, allowing me to channel my pain outward. At school, my inability to control my emotions made me lash out. I will never forget the day I hurled scissors toward a girl who had been taunting me, her insults cutting through my already fragile state. It was not enough; I grabbed a chair and warned her, "This time, I won't miss." My teacher's swift intervention stopped me from a decision I would regret.

I never told my family about the bullying; I could not. I was convinced that no one would care or help, so I shut down. My mother's eventual discovery of what I had endured left her heartbroken, but by then, it was too late. I had lost myself in a whirlwind of rage and anger management classes.

Therapy became an outlet for emotions I did not realize I was still carrying. My therapist placed a punching bag in front of me, plastered with the names of those who had hurt me—bullies, my father, and everyone who contributed to my torment. The emotions resurfaced, and as I pummeled the bag, I unleashed years of buried anger. My fists were not just hitting the fabric—they were tearing through years of neglect, pain, and betrayal.

In that room, I became a storm—uncontrollable, destructive, and consumed by my own fury. My therapist saw it; the school saw it. But no one understood the source of my rage or the battles I fought every day to suppress it.

Roots of My Trauma

The roots of my trauma stretch deep into my childhood, back to the painful memories of fights with Joe, who often provoked me for his own amusement. In every battle, he claimed to be teaching me lessons, but the lessons I learned were far from what he intended. These fights left me with the twisted belief that it was acceptable for a man to lay firsthand a woman even if that man was your own father if he justified it with an "I love you."

The culmination of this torment happened when I was seventeen. Joe punched me in the eye, leaving it black and swollen for three agonizing days. That single punch was more than just physical pain, it symbolized all the years of abuse and manipulation. Afterward, I was sent to stay with my Aunt Sarah and Uncle Frank for a week. The entire experience left me wounded and confused, as I tried to make sense of why I had been subjected to such cruelty. The love I once held for my father had morphed into an intense and enduring hatred.

During that final confrontation, something in me snapped. I fought back not just physically, but emotionally. In that moment, I felt like I had won the battle of the mind. The revenge I had been craving for so long was finally mine. But even in that victory, my soul ached for comfort. I longed for my grandmother's embrace, her warmth, and the safety I once felt in her arms, as the emotional storm inside me raged on.

The Illusion of Popularity and Toxic Love

Changing schools brought a whirlwind of emotions, a blend of hope, dread, and uncertainty. On the one hand, I saw it as a chance to leave behind the ghosts of my past and start over. I had been desperate to escape the suffocating environment of my old school, where memories of pain and rejection clung to me like shadows. But the trauma did not disappear when I packed my bags and walked into the halls of a new building. Instead, it followed me, lurking beneath the surface, coloring every interaction with fear and anger. I had not just left one painful chapter behind; I was carrying the weight of it into the next.

At my new school, the unfamiliar faces and the new surroundings offered a glimmer of hope. This time things will be different. This unfamiliar environment would allow me to find the love and acceptance I had been longing for since my father walked out of my life. But hope quickly turned into a toxic search for validation. My desperation for connection blinded me to the red flags around me, and I latched onto relationships that were more harmful than healing. I believed that if someone could just love me, anyone, it would fill the gaping hole in my heart. This mindset sets the stage for new struggles that would deepen my pain.

To my surprise, I gained popularity quickly. But it was not the kind of popularity that made me feel good about myself; it was shallow, built on a foundation of desperation rather than true connection. I craved attention like a drug, seeking to fill the void left by my father's absence. Popularity became my coping mechanism, a way to distract myself from the rejection and abandonment that still haunted me. But as I climbed the social ladder, I realized that it was not making me feel better; instead, it was amplifying my sense of worthlessness. The attention I received never filled the emptiness; it just masked it temporarily, leaving me hollower than before.

Relationships became my new battleground. My first serious boyfriend, Tyler, seemed to be the answer to my prayers at first. He gave me the affection and validation I had longed for, temporarily filling the emotional gaps that my father had left behind. I felt fixed, believing that this relationship would finally give me the security I craved. But six months in, Tyler shattered my trust by cheating on me. The betrayal was gut-wrenching, but instead of walking away, I accepted it as just another wound in an extensive line of hurt. I was so numb to the idea of being treated poorly that I did not even flinch when he broke my heart. It felt like confirmation of what deep down that I was not worth being loved properly.

By the time I turned sixteen, I was trapped in a destructive cycle of toxic relationships. Tyler continued to cheat on me, each betrayal cutting deeper than the last. Every time I discovered his infidelity, my self-esteem plummeted even further. I convinced myself that I was not deserving of fidelity, love, or respect. It became a twisted routine: he would cheat, I would confront him, we would argue, and then I would take him back, hoping that this time he would change. But deep down, I knew he would not. The cycle of infidelity and reconciliation became my reality, and with every round, I found myself sinking deeper into a pit of self-loathing.

As my anger festered, I became someone I barely recognized. I started lashing out at Tyler and others, spewing venomous words to shield myself from more pain. I thought that by being verbally abusive, by being the one to inflict hurt, I could somehow regain control of my life. But all I was doing was mirroring the very pain that had been inflicted on me. I had absorbed the toxicity around me, and in my desperation to protect myself, I had become toxic too.

The anger that once simmered beneath the surface now boiled over. I was quick to snap at the smallest light, my patience worn thin by years of unresolved hurt. I pushed people away before they had a chance to hurt me, building walls so high that I could not even see over them. My relationships were fraught with tension, and I often found myself walking the fine line between love and hate. The emotional wounds that my father's abandonment had left in my heart manifested in my interactions with others, particularly in my relationship with Tyler. He became the target of my anger, my verbal outbursts, and my distrust, even though I knew deep down that the real issue ran much deeper than his infidelity.

PAIN RAISED ME: BUT TRAUMA HEALED ME

It was during this time that I began to recognize the destructive patterns into which I had fallen. I could see how the pain from my past was shaping my present, how my desperation for love and acceptance had led me into relationships that only caused more harm. I started to understand that the validation I was seeking from others would never be enough to heal the wounds inside me. But even with this realization, I did not know how to break free from the cycle. It felt like I was trapped in an endless loop of pain and anger, with no obvious way out.

Looking back now, I can see that this period of my life was a pivotal turning point. It was the moment when I began to realize that true healing could not come from external sources; it had to come from within. The relationships I had relied on to fill the void left by my father's absence were only temporary fixes for a much deeper wound. It would take years before I fully understood this before I would learn to stop seeking validation in others and start finding it in God's unconditional love. But this realization marked the beginning of that journey, the first step toward healing, self-discovery, and reclaiming my worth.

Becoming a Predator

In my pursuit of power and control, I transformed into someone I no longer recognized. Once vulnerable and open, the girl who sought love and acceptance now evolved into a figure driven by revenge, consumed by the need to regain control over the hurt that had plagued me. I studied men's desires, learning how to manipulate them as they had manipulated me. It became my armor, a defense mechanism designed to shield me from the possibility of more pain. Every interaction was a calculated move, each step carefully planned to keep me ahead in the game of emotional warfare. The girl who had once been so full of hope had become a predator.

It was no longer about love; it was about control. In relationships, I made sure that I was the one pulling the strings. I would flatter, charm, and play the role of the perfect companion until I had them hooked. Then, just when they thought they had me, I would switch, revealing the cold, detached person I had become. They were left confused, hurt, and questioned about what they had done wrong. But in my mind, it was all justified. It was a way to make sure I would never be hurt again. The power I held over them was intoxicating, filling the void left by the pain of my past.

I had mastered the rules of this twisted game. I became proficient at reading their insecurities and vulnerabilities. My words, once soft and compassionate, now carried a sharp edge, capable of cutting deep without hesitation. If they tried to get close, I would have put up walls so high they could not climb them. Trust had become a foreign concept to me, and I lived in a constant state of suspicion. I did not want anyone to get too close, because deep down, I believed they would eventually betray me, just like everyone else.

Good men crossed my path who genuinely wanted to care for me, who saw the broken parts of me and still wanted to help. But I pushed them away. I hurt them before they could hurt me. In my mind, it was better to destroy the relationship on my terms than to allow them to have the power to walk away and leave me shattered. I had convinced myself that no one could understand the extent of my trauma, that no man could ever fully comprehend the depth of my pain and the reasons behind my destructive behavior.

Lyrica Anderson's song, do not Take It Personal, became my anthem. It was a song that perfectly captured my mindset. I did not mean to break hearts, but I could not help it. The damage done to me had turned me into someone who could not love, not genuinely. The song's lyrics spoke to the truth I lived every day: I did not want to hurt others, but I could not stop myself. It was the only way I knew to protect myself. The satisfaction of causing others the pain I had once felt became my twisted form of healing. I thought that if I could make them feel just an ounce of what I had endured, it would somehow make my own pain more bearable.

But the reality was far from satisfying. With each heart I broke, I felt a deeper emptiness settle in. The temporary rush of power quickly faded, and I was left with nothing but the same wounds I had tried to coverup. I was stuck in a cycle of destruction, unable to break free. The predator I had become was trapped in a cage of her own making, haunted by the memories of who she used to be.

Chapter 3: Transitioning Into Adulthood – A Dangerous Journey of Self-Discovery

1 Corinthians 13:11 - "When I was a child, I talked like a child, I thought like a child, I reasoned like a child. When I became a man, I put the ways of childhood behind me.

As I transitioned into adulthood, I embarked on a journey of self-discovery, eager to embrace independence and freedom. The excitement of moving on from the confines of high school and stepping into the world of college brought with it a sense of thrill, a new chapter of life that promised growth and learning. But this newfound freedom carried a dangerous undertone. While I grew wiser in some respects, I was still blind to the simplicity of my thinking, making me vulnerable to deeper pain.

On the outside, it seemed like I had everything with me. I was making decisions, trying to build a life, and taking steps toward independence. But on the inside, I was fighting an ongoing battle with the demons of my trauma. Each day there was a dangerous balancing act between the excitement of freedom and the terror of uncertainty. I was constantly walking a fine line, one wrong step away from plunging into emotional chaos.

There were moments when the pain from my past felt unbearable, yet a twisted part of me found satisfaction in hurting others. It gave me a sense of control, a way to manage the hurt I could not escape from. This dangerous pattern of behavior consumed my life, and I feared my future, unsure of what lay ahead.

Looking back at my accomplishments, they amounted to nothing. Sure, I had graduated from high school and earned a spot on the second team all-district in softball, but in my mind, these achievements were insignificant. They could not heal the wounds that had been festering inside me for years. I had grown into an adult, but the ruthless, troubled teenager inside me had not matured. Instead, she had transformed into a lost and troubled young woman, still carrying the burdens of her past.

The Darkest Night

It was on one particularly dark night that I found myself at my lowest. The enemy whispered in my ear, telling me that I should end it all, that no one would care if I died. As I sat there, tormented by these thoughts, I could not help but wonder if the enemy was right. Part of me knew I did not want to die, but another part of me longed for the suffering to end. The idea of no longer feeling the weight of my pain, of finally escaping the trauma, was tempting.

I sat there, gripped by fear and despair, wrestling with the thought of ending my life. The enemy's words played over and over in my mind, filling me with doubt and hopelessness. But in that moment of deep torment, something shifted. I knew that I did not want to die. I wanted the pain to end, but I still had a sliver of hope left within me. Desperate for relief, I did the only thing I knew to do; I got on my knees and prayed.

That night, I begged God for divine intervention. I pleaded with Him to release me from the pain and trauma that had been inflicted upon me by my father and others who had hurt me. I cried out for healing and asked for guidance, knowing that if I did not receive help soon, I would be lost. I realized that I was slowly withering from the inside, my emotional and mental well-being already fractured beyond recognition.

A Glimmer of Hope

After that night, something began to shift. I started attending a new church, and for the first time in a long time, I felt a glimmer of hope. The church leaders welcomed me with open arms, and I developed a close connection with them, particularly with the First Lady. She became a motherly figure in my life, someone who offered the guidance and care I had longed for. She saw the broken pieces of my heart and, instead of judging me, she offered me unconditional love.

One Sunday, during a sermon titled No More Lip Service, my bishop's words resonated deeply within me. As I sat in the pew, listening to his message, it felt as if God Himself was speaking directly to me, urging me to take a step toward salvation and recovery.

The bishop's words hit me like a bolt of lightning, forcing me to reflect on the dangerous consequences of continuing down the dark path I was on. That very day, I made the decision to surrender my life to Christ. I could not keep living in the shadows, consumed by pain and anger. I needed to be free from the darkness that had gripped me for so long.

The Struggle to Adjust

Even though I had taken that crucial step toward healing, the transition was not easy. I had spent 22 years trapped in a cycle of trauma and pain, and suddenly, I found myself free from the source of that torment. It felt liberating, yet confusing. I did not know how to manage the freedom for which I had longed. The ability to come and go as I pleased, to live my life without fear of my father, was something I had dreamed of for years. The idea of being "grown" and independent was thrilling, and I fantasized about all the possibilities this new life would offer me.

But with that freedom came new challenges for which I was not prepared. My mother, who had always been there to warn me and guide me, saw the dangerous path I was on. She warned me repeatedly to be careful, but in my youthful arrogance, I could not see her concern for what it was. To me, it felt like she was trying to hold me back, to keep me from living in the fantasy world I had created for myself. The more she tried to guide me, the more frustrated I became.

I felt like I had been trapped for so long, living a life I had not asked for, and now that I was free, I did not want anyone to tell me what to do. I was determined to prove everyone wrong, to show them that I could live my life on my own terms. But my mother's love, no matter how pure, became an obstacle in my eyes. The more love she showed, the angrier I became. Disrespect, once an infrequent occurrence, became my weapon. I aimed it at those closest to me, especially her.

The Wounds of Resentment

As I navigated my growing anger and confusion, I found myself questioning the decisions of those around me, particularly my mother. I struggled to understand how she had allowed certain painful experiences to unfold. At times, my mind wandered to dark places, wondering if she truly grasped the depth of my suffering. However, deep down, I knew she cared. It was my own pain that twisted these thoughts, pushing me into a mindset where it was finally my turn to live on my terms, regardless of the consequences. This idea of taking control became my armor, shielding me from further vulnerability, but at the cost of those I cared about.

Her words of concern and advice became unbearable. I avoided coming home as much as possible, isolating myself from her and from everyone who cared about me. I did not want to face the truth—that I was still hurting, still broken, and that the path I was on was not leading to the healing I needed.

Chapter 4 - He is Him, but Not Him: The Reflection of My Father

Ephesians 6:4 - "Fathers, do not exasperate your children; instead, bring them up in the training and instruction of the Lord."

The Search for Love and Acceptance

In my early twenties, I still had not figured out what it meant to be in a healthy relationship. I was never shown how a man is supposed to treat a woman, or how a woman is supposed to reciprocate that love. It felt like I was always left to figure it out on my own. Time after time, the men I dated shared characteristics with my father. Whether the resemblance was small or large, there was always something that reminded me of him.

Each time I thought I had found someone different; it was as if I was blind to the reality that they, too, carried the same qualities. One man mirrored my father exactly. He lied, cheated, and even stole, all while claiming to love me. It baffled me—how could I not see these traits right away? I had endured with my father, I should have been able to recognize the signs, but I did not. Instead, I was searching for something deeper: the love I had never received from my father.

Despite God blessing me with a father figure in my Uncle Don, I still craved that paternal love from a man. Even though I had accepted Christ into my life, I was not fully trusting God to fill that void. I felt like I needed a man to make me feel whole, to somehow heal the wounds caused by another man. But as much as I yearned for it, it only led me down paths of confusion and disappointment.

Daddy Issues and Unhealthy Patterns

My unresolved "daddy issues" continued to play out in every relationship. I could never seem to find what I wanted. Insecurities plagued me—I constantly wondered if I was enough. I compared myself to other women, thinking I was not as beautiful, was not doing what they were doing, and it drove me into deeper self-doubt. The painful memory of my father pretending to have another daughter would always resurface, making me feel like there was something inherently wrong with me.

With each failed relationship, I carried more baggage into the next. I expected something different, yet always ended up with the same result. I placed pressures on these men that they could not bear. I wanted them to carry a weight that only God could hold, and I held them to a standard they could never live up to.

This pursuit of love and acceptance drove me to explore more dangerous avenues. I turned to dating apps, desperate to find what I had never received from my father. But in these encounters, I was emotionally guarded. I refused to let anyone truly know me, building walls that I would not let anyone tear down. I was not allowing God to govern my decisions, instead becoming my own guide, making choices based on my feelings rather than His wisdom.

The Date That Changed Everything

One day, I went on a date with a guy I barely knew. He seemed nice, and I was eager to see where this potential relationship could lead. Despite warnings from others about his questionable character, I dismissed their concerns. I told myself, "I'm grown," and ignored the tugging of the Holy Spirit.

At first, the date seemed to go well, but something fell off. I could not place it. He was a gentleman, not acting like the men I had experienced before. However, as the night unfolded, things took a sudden and terrifying turn. Later that night, we went back to his apartment, and while everything seemed normal, I could not shake the uneasy feeling in my gut. Still, I ignored it.

We shared a kiss, which quickly escalated into something more. He wanted to go further, but I hesitated. I told him to stop, but fueled by passion, he kept advancing. Fear and confusion washed over me as I realized how easily he had switched from being polite to predatory. He was a wolf in sheep's clothing, focused on one thing: getting what he wanted, regardless of my consent.

Fight or Flight

In that moment, all my defenses came crumbling down. The word "no" held no weight to him, and I suddenly understood the gravity of the situation. My mind raced back to all the times I had to fight for myself, knowing that no one was coming to save me. I had seen scenes like this on TV, where someone came to rescue the girl, but I knew that was rare. No one was coming for me, I had to fight.

I began to fight and push, even though I knew I could not physically overpower the man. I still aimed to make the struggle more challenging for him. My mind drifted to the story of the woman with the issue of blood. For twelve years, and how she had suffered but when she heard that Jesus was coming, she was certain he could heal her. Driven by determination, she knew that if she could just touch the hem of his garment, she would be healed. I understood that I might not win this immediate battle, but I was focused on winning the larger war.

I told myself that if I could just reach the hallway, I would find the help I needed. The fight to get to the door felt like it was happening in slow motion, and success seemed almost impossible. But I kept fighting, visualizing how the woman with the issue of blood had pressed through the crowd with unwavering focus. Her goal was clear: to reach Jesus, no matter what. If she had to walk, she would walk. If she had to run, she would run. If she had to crawl, she would crawl. The mere thought of her determination fueled my own resolve.

My singular focus became getting to the hallway by any means necessary. Eventually, I reached the door and made it to the hallway. But once there, I froze, as if all my strength had drained away.

The Aftermath

He tried to blame me for what had happened, saying the kiss was my fault, but I knew better. I had said no—he just did not listen. I was left wondering if anyone would believe me if I spoke up. I had willingly gone to his apartment, and I knew people would judge me for that. But after seeking advice, I decided to tell my story.

That night, I tossed and turned in bed, still in shock. I felt embarrassed, weak, and utterly defeated. It reminded me of the helpless girl I had been in high school, the one who had promised herself she would never allow something like this to happen. But now, there was a bigger hole in my heart, one that left me feeling even more lost and confused.

The once loving little girl who had been full of hope was now trapped in her own darkness. I could not find my way back, and the tunnel of despair only seemed to grow longer. I was drowning in it, unsure if I could ever understand something clearly again.

Chapter 5: Wrestling with the Darkness

Ephesians 6:12 - For we do not wrestle against flesh and blood, but against principalities, against powers, against the rulers of [the darkness of this age, against spiritual *hosts* of wickedness in the heavenly *places*.

Drowning in Darkness

The darkness inside me was overwhelming, suffocating. It consumed every part of my being, and I did not.

know how to escape. Processing the trauma that clung to me like a second skin felt impossible, so I sought anything that could numb the pain. I became reckless, turning to violence, anger, and the wrong company for comfort. These dark companions fed my inner turmoil, masking the deep ache I felt but never truly soothing it. Music, once a source of comfort, now only filled the empty spaces of my soul, but even that was not enough to silence the internal storm. I craved an escape, something that would give me a temporary excuse from the relentless emotional pain.

That is when I found myself in clubs, surrounded by people who had only one goal in mind, having a suitable time. The neon lights, the pulsing music, and the carefree attitudes offered temporary refuge. For a fleeting moment, which is all I needed too: just a fun time, a release from reality, a chance to feel happy even if it was only for a few hours. In those moments, I thought I had found my answer. I wanted to be anywhere but in the confines of my own mind, where the pain lingered.

At first, the partying seemed to help. The energy of the crowd filled me with an artificial sense of peace, a buzz of distraction that allowed me to forget the heavy weight of my past. But as time went on, I started to need it increasingly. The heights were short lived, and the fleeting joy

I experienced quickly faded. Soon, I was chasing after that temporary relief like an addict, going out night after night, seeking distractions that would drown out the pain I did not know how to face. But in trying to escape, I only lost myself deeper in the darkness.

Losing the Battle of Drinking and Smoking

When the thrill of partying was not enough to dull the pain, I turned to drinking and smoking. I thought it would be a way to cope, a way to escape further. I remembered seeing my father battle these same demons, watching him spiral down a similar path. Yet, I convinced myself I was different, that I could control it, that it would not take over my life the way it had him. At first, it seemed harmless. I drank casually, socially, and vaped here and there. It felt like I was just having fun, that I was still in control.

But before I knew it, these habits became my crutches. Whenever I felt scared, triggered, or overwhelmed by emotions I did not know how to process, I ran to my vape, seeking comfort in a cloud of smoke. When the pain had been burying for so long started creeping back, I drowned it out with alcohol, numbing myself to the reality I refused to face. I remember the first time I got drunk. It was like I returned from a long five-year trip, and everything around me felt surreal, like the world had slowed down and I was floating above it all, detached from reality. For a moment, I thought I had found peace.

But the next morning, the harsh sunlight spilling into my room felt invasive, like a spotlight revealing everything I had tried to hide. Every noise was an assault on the fragile sense of peace I thought I had found the night before. I felt confused, disoriented, and uncertain—unsure whether to run from or dive deeper into the haze that alcohol provided. Part of me knew that this was not the answer, but another part was so desperate to escape that I did not care.

Before long, social drinking became something more. I was no longer drinking to enjoy a night out. I was drinking to chase that momentary relief, to numb the pain that was always lurking just beneath the surface.

Smoking became a routine, something I turned to whenever the darkness inside me felt too overwhelming. I convinced myself I could always stop, that I could turn back whenever I wanted. But with every wrong choice, I was only sinking deeper, distancing myself from God, the only One who absolutely loved me.

A Moment of Crisis

One day, after weeks of heavy drinking and smoking, I found myself at a homecoming tailgate. I was already weighted down by a criminal court case and the crushing weight of my emotions. Desperate for an escape, Accepted drinks from strangers, something I had been raised never to do. I did not care anymore; I just wanted to forget. After the tailgate, I went out to eat with friends, trying to keep up appearances, but as the night went on, I knew something was wrong. The world around me started to spin, and I felt like I was losing control of myself and my surroundings.

I remember feeling disconnected from reality, barely holding on. Against better judgment, I drove myself home, trying to make sense of the hallucinations that were flooding my mind. I called a friend, slurring my words, telling her that the floor was moving, that I could not hold on much longer. She was terrified for me, and while she stayed on the line, trying to keep me alert, she called my Aunt Gladys to check on me. By the time my aunt arrived, I was barely able to stand. I could hear her banging at the door, calling my name, but I was so close to giving up. Part of me wanted to fight, but another part of me felt like there was no point. It felt like the pain, the trauma, everything I had been running from had finally caught up with me.

Drowning in My Pain

I felt like I was drowning, not just at that moment but in all the years of unresolved trauma. My aunt called 911, but before she could explain my condition, the operator told her that an ambulance was already on its way. Even though I thought it was the end for me, God had other plans. I do not remember much after that just waking up in a hospital bed, surrounded by my family, all of them praying for me.

That night in the hospital, as I stared up at the ceiling, I began questioning everything. I had given my life to Christ; however, I wondered how I ended up here? Why had I fallen so deep into darkness? It reminded me of Peter walking on water, sinking when he took his eyes off Jesus. I had let the enemy deceive me into thinking the world's distractions could bring me peace. I had turned away from the One who loved me most, and now I was drowning. But just when I thought it was too late, I called out to Jesus, and He rescued me, just as He had done for Peter.

A Turning Point

As I reflected on that night, I realized how every decision I had made led me to that moment. I had run so far from God, but He had never left me. In every poor choice, He was there, offering me a way out. In every moment of loneliness, He reminded me that He was right beside me, waiting for me to turn back.

It was in that hospital bed that I began to understand the depth of God's love. He had been with me through every trial, every mistake, and every dark moment. He had been calling me back to Him, waiting for me to surrender. It made me think of Matthew 11:28-29, where Jesus invites us to come to Him for rest. All along, I had been running from the very peace and rest that God was offering me. That night, I chose to stop running. That night, I decided to give Him control and let Him guide me out of the darkness.

God did not just save me from that moment of crisis He saved me from myself. He showed me that no matter how far I had fallen, His grace was enough to lift me back up. I was not just a survivor of trauma or a victim of my choices I was a child of God, redeemed and restored.

The Need for Forgiveness

As I continued to reflect on my journey, it became clear that something had to change. I could no longer live with the weight of my past dictating every step I took toward my future. My heart had been heavy for far too long, burdened by the pain of betrayal, abandonment, and fear. It was like carrying an invisible chain that constantly dragged me backward, preventing me from fully stepping into the life God had planned for me. I realized that, if I wanted to be free, I needed to confront the one thing I had been avoiding: forgiveness.

The first person I knew I had to forgive was my father. For years, I had been running from the pain of his absence, masking it with anger and bitterness. I convinced myself that I was justified in holding onto that resentment, but in truth, it was eating away at me. My father's actions, or lack thereof, had left a deep wound in my heart, one that I thought time alone could heal. But as the years passed, the pain only seemed to grow, festering into something that clouded every relationship I had, even my relationship with God.

I had to stop running from my past and face it head-on. The truth is forgiveness is not about forgetting or excusing the wrongs done to us it is about releasing the hold that those wrongs have on our hearts. I came to understand that forgiveness was the only way to move forward, not just for my father's sake, but for my own healing and peace of mind. By clinging to bitterness, I was giving power to the very pain I wanted to escape from. I had to let go, not because it was easy, but because it was necessary for my freedom.

The words of Mark 11:26 echoed in my mind: "But if you do not forgive, neither will your Father in heaven forgive your trespasses." This verse shook me to my core. It was not just about what had been done to me it was about my relationship with God. How could I expect to receive His forgiveness if I refused to offer it to others? The realization hit me hard if I held onto this pain, I would never fully experience God's grace. His forgiveness was freely given, but it required me to release the chains of unforgiveness I had wrapped so tightly around my heart.

Forgiving my father was only the first step. There were others I needed to release from the prison of my anger, people whose actions had left lasting scars. The man who nearly took something valuable from me I had buried that memory deep, hoping it would fade with time, but it continued to resurface, reminding me of the fear and vulnerability I had felt. It was an event that had left me feeling powerless, and for years I let that feeling dictate my sense of worth. I had allowed his actions to define me, but no more.

In forgiving him, I was not condoning what he had done or pretending that the trauma had not occurred. Instead, I was choosing to reclaim the power I had lost. I was deciding that he would no longer have control over my thoughts, my emotions, or my future. Forgiveness was my way of saying that what had been taken from me would not define the rest of my life. It was a declaration of victory, a refusal to let my past be the lens through which I viewed the world.

Forgiving was not an overnight process. It did not come without tears or moments of doubt. I had to continually remind myself that forgiveness was not a feeling but a decision, a decision I had to make daily.

There were times when the anger would resurface, and I would have to surrender it to God, asking Him to help me let go, once again. Through prayer and reflection, I learned that forgiveness was a process of surrender, not just of the pain but of the need for justice, the desire for revenge, and the hope for closure that I had been holding onto.

As I released each person who had hurt me, I felt something shifting within me. My heart, once so heavy with pain, began to feel lighter. The chains that had once bound me so tightly were breaking, one by one. I could finally see that forgiveness was not for them; it was for me. It was the key that unlocked the door to my healing. It was what allowed me to move from being a victim of my circumstances to a victor in Christ.

Through this journey of forgiveness, I learned that I was no longer defined by what had been done to me, but by who I was in Christ, a child of God, redeemed, loved, and free. The past would always be a part of my story, but it no longer had to dictate my future. As I forgave, I stepped into the fullness of God's forgiveness, grace, and healing, ready to embrace the victorious life He had planned for me all along.

A New Beginning

One morning, I woke up with an overwhelming sense of heaviness. The weight of my pain felt unbearable, and I knew I needed to do something different. Without thinking, I dropped to my knees and poured my heart out to God, tears streaming down my face. I cried out in desperation, asking Him the question that had haunted me for so long: "Why, God? Why did You allow me to go through so much pain? Why did You let my life unravel the way it did?"

The room was quiet, except for the sound of my own sobs. I waited, hoping for an answer, some sign that God would speak to me in that moment and reveal the reason for all the suffering I had endured. But as the seconds passed, I heard nothing. The silence felt deafening, and for a moment, I wondered if God had heard me at all.

Still, I refused to give up. I reached for my Bible, my hands trembling, and opened it. My eyes landed on a passage in Romans 8:28: "And we know that in all things, God works for the good of those who love him, who have been called according to his purpose." The words hit me like a wave, washing over me, and in that instant, I knew that God had spoken not through an audible voice but through His Word. He did not give me a direct answer to my "why," but instead, He reminded me of His promise.

In that moment, something shifted. My heart, which had been so full of doubt and pain, began to soften. I did not question Him anymore. I did not need to. For the first time in a long time, I trusted Him. Even though I did not understand the purpose behind my suffering, I realized that God did. He was working behind the scenes, orchestrating something far greater than I could imagine.

From that day forward, God began to take me through a season of obedience—a season that required me to fully surrender my will to His. It was not easy. There were days when I still struggled with fear and doubt, days when I questioned whether God truly had a plan for me. But in those moments of weakness, He would gently remind me that His ways were higher than mine. Every time I turned to Him, whether in prayer or through scripture, I was met with a quiet assurance that He was with me, guiding me through the storm.

Through this season, God showed me that faithfulness was not about understanding everything He was doing in my life; it was about trusting that He was in control, even when things did not make sense. It was about taking the next step, even when the path ahead seemed uncertain. He taught me that obedience required patience, humility, and a willingness to let go of my need for answers.

Slowly, I began to see that God had never left me—not in my darkest moments, not even when I had turned my back on Him in anger and frustration. He had been there all along, waiting for me to return, patiently calling me back to His arms. The peace I had been searching for was not something I had to earn or chase after; it was already available to me in Him. I just had to let go of my need to control the narrative of my life and trust that His plan was better than anything I could ever write for myself.

As I leaned into this season of obedience, I started to notice subtle but powerful changes in my heart. The bitterness that had once consumed me began to fade. The resentment I had felt toward God and others was replaced by a quiet, steady faith. I learned that trusting God was not about expecting life to be perfect or pain-free; it was about believing that no matter what happened, He was working all things for my good.

God was teaching me that every tear I had cried, every heartache I had endured, and every moment of suffering had a purpose. He was using those painful experiences to shape me, to refine me, and to draw me closer to Him. And while I did not have all the answers to the "why," I no longer needed them. I had far greater faith in His goodness and a deep sense of peace that only comes from surrendering my life to Him.

In time, I realized that this season of obedience was not just a test of my faith, but a gift. It was God's way of drawing me closer, teaching me to rely on Him completely, and showing me that His plans for me were filled with hope, even when the road seemed unclear. It was through this season that I began to experience the peace I had been longing for the peace that surpasses all understanding, the peace that only comes from walking in step with God.

Chapter 6: Rebuilding Trust – From Victim to Victor

Romans 8:37- Yet in all these things we are more than conquerors through Him who loved us.

The journey from victimhood to victory is neither quick nor linear. It is a winding road filled with moments of intense introspection, struggle, and profound revelation. This path is not one of immediate relief or simple solutions, but rather, it is an ongoing process that challenges your deepest fears, breaks down your most firmly held beliefs, and reshapes how you see yourself, your pain, and the world around you.

In the aftermath of trauma, there is a tendency to believe that healing is a straight line from hurt to recovery. But I soon discovered that this was far from the truth. Healing is messy. There are days when you feel as though you have made progress, only to find yourself unexpectedly spiraling back into old fears, doubts, and insecurities. The weight of your past can reemerge, gripping you in moments when you least expect it. In those moments, it is easy to feel defeated, as if your trauma has an unrelenting hold over you.

As I began my own journey of healing, I quickly realized that it was not just about recovering from the traumatic events themselves. The real work lay in addressing the deeper wounds that trauma had left behind—the ones that had shaped my sense of self-worth, my ability to trust, and my relationship with God. These were not surface-level scars; they ran deep, buried in the core of who I had become. It was as though trauma had rewired my entire way of being, making me believe I was defined by the pain I had endured.

At the outset, my mind was a battlefield of conflicting emotions. On one hand, I wanted desperately to heal and move forward. On the other hand, the pain was so familiar that part of me clung to it, as if letting go would mean losing a part of myself. This emotional tug-of-war made the journey even more complicated. I would take one step forward only to feel pulled two steps back, and with each setback, my frustration grew. It became apparent that healing would require more than just time; it would demand patience, self-compassion, and perseverance.

Introspection has become a key part of the healing process. I had to sit with my emotions, something I had spent years avoiding. The pain was intense, but it forced me to confront the unresolved feelings I had buried deep inside. I reflected on the trauma itself, yes, but also on the emotional and mental patterns that had taken root in my life because of it. How had these experiences shaped my perception of myself? How had they influenced the way I interacted with the world? Most importantly, how had they affected my relationship with God?

This process was agonizing at times because it meant revisiting some of the most painful moments of my life. But it was in those moments of deep introspection that I began to uncover profound truths about myself. I learned that while trauma had broken parts of me, it had also revealed strengths I never knew I possessed. I started to see that the wounds I carried did not have to define me. Instead, they could serve as catalysts for growth and transformation.

The struggle, however, did not end there. Healing was not just about reflection; it also required action. I had to actively work to rebuild trust in myself, a task that seemed impossible after years of feeling broken and unworthy. Trauma had stripped away my confidence, leaving me doubting every decision I made, every emotion I felt. I questioned whether I was capable of healing, of moving forward, of truly becoming whole again. Rebuilding trust in myself was the hardest part of the journey. It required me to not only forgive myself for the ways I had reacted to the trauma but also to believe that I was worthy of healing in the first place.

Once I began to rebuild that trust in myself, the next step was to extend it outward. Trusting others, after being hurt so deeply, felt like walking onto a battlefield unarmed. I struggled with the fear of being vulnerable again, of opening myself up to the possibility of getting hurt. But through time, prayer, and therapy, I realized that rebuilding trust was not about placing my faith blindly in others. Instead, it was about setting boundaries, listening to my instincts, and allowing myself to be vulnerable to people who had earned my trust. It was about learning that not everyone would hurt me and that I had the power to choose who I let into my life.

The final and most transformative part of my journey was rebuilding my trust in God. Trauma has a way of shaking your faith to its core. It can make you question why God allowed certain things to happen or whether He was even there at all. I had spent years wrestling with these questions, unsure of how to reconcile my faith with the pain I had endured. But as I journeyed through my healing, I came to realize that God had never left me, even in the darkest moments of my life. He had been with me all along, guiding me, comforting me, and waiting for me to turn to Him.

Rebuilding trust in God did not mean that I suddenly understood why everything had happened, nor did it erase the pain of the past. But it did mean that I could lean on Him for strength, even when I did not have all the answers. It meant that I could surrender the weight of my trauma to Him, trusting that He would continue to guide me through the process of healing. Slowly but surely, I began to see that healing was not something I had to do on my own; it was something God wanted to walk through with me, step by step.

Through this journey of rebuilding trust in myself, others, and God, I came to a powerful revelation: healing is not a destination, but a lifelong process. There is no point at which you can declare yourself fully healed, fully whole, fully free from the past. Instead, healing is something you must continually nurture, much like a garden. There will be days when you feel strong and resilient, and there will be days when the old wounds ache, when you feel as though you are back at square one. And that is okay. Because within every wound lies the potential for growth, for resilience, and for triumph.

What I have learned is that healing is not about erasing the past but about transforming the way you carry it. It is about finding the strength to keep moving forward, even when the road is steep and uncertain. It is about recognizing that pain does not have to define you, but it can shape you in ways that make you stronger, wiser, and more compassionate. The journey from victim to victor is ongoing, but with each step, I have discovered a deeper understanding of myself and a profound sense of victory that comes not from the absence of pain but from the resilience and faith that have grown from it.

The Haunting Shadows of the Courtroom

In the initial stages of healing, I felt overwhelmed by the weight of my past. The courtroom was not just a place of legal proceedings; it became a haunting reminder of the night that had shattered my sense of safety. I had to face the trauma in a setting where I felt vulnerable and exposed. Although I was no longer physically bound by the events that had transpired, my mind remained imprisoned, locked in a cycle of fear and insecurity. Every step I took forward seemed to be met with an invisible force pulling me back.

The courtroom experience forced me to relive the trauma repeatedly, each time chipping away at the fragile sense of self I was trying to rebuild. The legal system, while seeking justice, inadvertently tethered me to the very pain I was trying to escape. I realized that despite having survived the event, I had yet to break free from the emotional and mental strengths that it had created within me.

The Victim Mentality

During this tumultuous period, it became clear to me that my self-perception as a victim was deeply intertwined with my understanding of self-worth. I had grown accustomed to seeing myself through the lens of the suffering I had endured, defining my entire identity by the pain of my past. I viewed my experiences as a life sentence, a burden I would have to carry forever. The idea of ever feeling free or worthy again seemed impossible.

But as I began to reflect on these beliefs, I started to recognize the flaws in my thinking. I had accepted the victim mentality as my truth, but God was calling me to something greater. He was urging me to shift my perspective, to see beyond the scars and understand that my worth was not determined by the trauma I had experienced, but by His love and purpose for my life. This revelation marked the beginning of a crucial turning point in my healing journey.

A New Identity in Christ

One of the most transformative moments in my life came when I encountered the truth of my identity in Christ. I began to internalize the powerful message that I was not defined by my past; rather, I was a child of God, created for a purpose, and destined for victory. Through scripture and prayer, I started to see myself not as a victim but as a victor, a person who had not only survived trauma but had been empowered by faith to rise above it.

As I studied passages like Romans 8:37, which declares, "In all these things we are more than conquerors through Him who loved us," I realized that God had already declared victory over my life. It was up to me to embrace it. I began to shed the labels I had placed on myself—the labels of broken, unworthy, and damaged—and replaced them with affirmations of my new identity in Christ: whole, loved, and victorious.

Rebuilding Trust in Myself

Rebuilding trust in myself after trauma was a painstaking and deeply personal journey, one that required me to look inward in ways I had never anticipated. When the trauma first struck, it shattered not only my external world but also the internal compass I had relied on to navigate life. I found myself constantly second-guessing every decision I made, doubting the validity of my own emotions, and questioning whether I could make choices that would lead me toward healing. My self-trust, once an innate part of who I was, had been fractured, leaving me in a state of confusion and uncertainty.

A Broken Compass

Every time I tried to decide—whether to be big or small—I felt paralyzed by fear. What if I chose wrong? What if I was leading myself down another path of pain or disappointment? Even in moments where I wanted to lean into healing, I found myself questioning whether I deserved it, or if it was even possible for me. It was not just my sense of confidence that had been shaken; it was my very ability to trust that I could guide myself to a better place.

This lack of self-trust was not just a byproduct of the trauma itself, but also the result of the negative beliefs I had formed about myself in the wake of it. I began to believe that I was somehow at fault for what had happened, that I had made choices that led me into harm's way. This self-blame festered within me, reinforcing the narrative that I was unworthy, incapable, and irreparably broken. With every misstep, these lies were confirmed, deepening the chasm between who I had been and who I now saw myself to be.

Examining the Wounds

Healing required more than just moving forward; it demanded that I stop and examine these wounds carefully. This meant not only confronting the trauma itself but also peeling back the layers of negative beliefs I had internalized about my worth, my identity, and my ability to recover. It was not an effortless process, but I uncovered I wanted to reopen an old scar, exposing the raw pain that lay beneath. But I knew that if I wanted to truly heal, I had to address these lies head-on.

I had to face the insidious belief that I was responsible for the pain I had endured. For so long, I had carried the weight of guilt, believing that if I had acted differently or been more vigilant, the trauma might have been avoided. But this was a lie. As I started to process what had happened, I realized that blaming myself only kept me trapped in the past, preventing me from stepping into the freedom I so desperately needed.

Replacing Lies with God's Truth

Each time I confronted one of these lies, I knew I could not just leave a void where that belief had been. I had to fill that space with something stronger, something true. That truth came from God. With every lie I dismantled, I replaced it with the truth of who I was in His eyes.

Where I was unworthy, I now declared that I was loved unconditionally. Scriptures like Psalm 139 reminded me that I was "fearfully and wonderfully made," not broken or beyond repair. Where I was responsible for my own pain, I began to see that I was not defined by the circumstances or choices of the past, but by the grace of God that covered me in the present.

Through prayer, meditation, and studying God's word, I began to reclaim my sense of self. I learned that trusting myself did not mean relying on my own strength alone—it meant trusting the God within me, the Holy Spirit guiding my steps. As I embraced His truth, I started to feel my confidence slowly return, not in an arrogant way but in a peaceful assurance that I could make decisions that would lead me toward healing, wholeness, and restoration.

The Unfolding Process

This process of rebuilding self-trust was not instantaneous. It took time and patience. There were moments when I stumbled and doubted again, but each time, I returned to the truth. I allowed myself to feel the discomfort of growth, knowing that healing required me to sit with the pain long enough to transform it.

As I journeyed deeper into this process, I began to realize that trusting myself was not just about making decisions. It was about believing that I was worthy of a better life, worthy of healing, and worthy of God's love. It was about trusting that the broken pieces of my life could be mended, not through my own efforts alone, but through a divine process of grace, redemption, and renewal.

In the end, I did not just regain trust in myself; I discovered a deeper trust in God's ability to lead me through the darkest valleys and into the light of a new day. Every step I took on the path of healing was a testament to that trust, and every small victory became a reminder that I was not a victim of my circumstances, but a victor through Christ's strength within me.

Trusting in God's Grace

One of the most significant steps in my journey was learning to trust in God's grace. For so long, I had struggled with feelings of guilt, shame, and unworthiness. I believed that my trauma and the mistakes I had made in the aftermath disqualified me from receiving God's love and forgiveness. But as I immersed myself in His word, I began to see that God's grace was far greater than anything I had done or experienced.

Isaiah 55:7-9 was instrumental in helping me understand this: "For my thoughts are not your thoughts, neither are your ways my ways, declares the Lord." His grace was abundant and unearned, and it was through this grace that I found the strength to forgive myself and move forward. I no longer had to carry the weight of guilt and self-blame; instead, I could rest in the knowledge that God had already forgiven me and was guiding me toward healing.

Forgiving Myself and Others

Forgiveness, particularly self-forgiveness, was one of the hardest but most necessary parts of my transformation. For years, I had carried the burden of self-blaming, believing that if I had done something different, the trauma could have been avoided. But through therapy and spiritual reflection, I began to understand that holding onto this guilt was not only unfair to myself but was also preventing me from fully stepping into the freedom God had for me.

As I forgave myself, I also found the strength to forgive those who had hurt me. Forgiveness did not mean excusing their actions, but it did mean releasing the hold that their actions had on my life. It meant choosing peace over bitterness and allowing God to heal the places where I had been wounded.

From Chains to Wings: A New Beginning

With every step I took in this journey from letting go of guilt to embracing my new identity in Christ—I began to see changes in my life. My confidence grew, and I started to notice opportunities for growth and healing that had previously seemed out of reach. I no longer viewed my past as a chain that held me back but as a testament to the resilience and strength that had been forged through my trials.

This chapter in my life was about more than just overcoming trauma—it was about embracing a new way of living. It was about recognizing my worth in God's eyes and stepping into the future with hope and faith.

Chapter 7: The Battle of the Mind: Therapy and Transformation

Romans 12:2- And do not be conformed to this world, but be transformed by the renewing of your mind, that you may prove what is that good and acceptable and perfect will of God."

Therapy often feels like a battleground, where the conflict is not with external enemies but with the deepest recesses of our own minds. It is a confrontation with the layers of emotional scars and subconscious patterns, many of which are shaped by past traumas. For me, this journey into therapy was nothing short of transformation, though it did not start that way. Initially, I entered it with reluctance, resistance, and a sense of skepticism. Yet over time, this journey evolved into one of profound self-discovery, healing, and growth. This chapter chronicles my personal experience with therapy, the hurdles, the breakthroughs, and the insights that turned this once-daunting process into a pathway toward renewal.

Therapy as Punishment

My relationship with therapy began on rocky terms. Growing up, therapy was introduced to me not as a healing tool, but as a form of punishment. It was not about uncovering my pain or working through my struggles; it was about managing my anger, a behavior that others found inconvenient or troubling. Each visit felt more like a reprimand, as if my emotions and outbursts were defects to be fixed rather than signs of something deeper. This early association left me jaded, viewing therapy as a place to vent, not to heal routine exercise in talking without solutions.

By the time I found myself sitting in Dr. Darren's office, I was already convinced it would be another hollow experience. My skepticism was palpable. I sat through the session with a closed heart and mind, eager for it to be over. But it was during that very first session that Dr. Darren posed a question that would shift my entire perspective: "Do you really want to change?"

At first, I bristled at the question, but it lingered in my thoughts long after the session ended. It forced me to confront the fact that my resistance was not to therapy itself, but to the vulnerability it demanded of me. Was I merely going through the motions, or was I truly ready to do the challenging work of change?

Confronting the Past

The real work of therapy began when I allowed myself to be fully present. Slowly, breakthrough moments began to emerge. One of the most profound moments came during a session where Dr. Darren guided me into a confrontation with my past, specifically the traumas of my childhood. It was not easy. In fact, I wanted to reopen old wounds, but this time with the purpose of finally allowing them to heal.

Dr. Darren's approach was meticulous yet compassionate. He helped me trace the roots of my anger and self-blame back to their origins, allowing me to see how much of my present struggles were echoes of unresolved pain. One exercise that changed everything for me was writing a letter to my younger self. The assignment seemed simple at first, but I avoided it for weeks, terrified of the emotions it might stir. Writing that letter meant facing the little girl inside me who had been neglected, misunderstood, and hurt.

When I finally mustered the courage to write, I discovered that the process was not about reliving the pain, but about offering that younger version of myself the reassurance and love she never received. It became an act of self-compassion, a way of releasing the grip of old traumas and opening the door to healing.

The Path to Self-Discovery

Through therapy, I began to uncover deep insights into the patterns that shaped my life. Dr. Darren helped me see that many of the behaviors and emotional struggles I had blamed myself for were conditioned responses to pain. They were not flaws in my character but survival mechanisms I had adopted in response to trauma.

This revelation was a game changer. I had spent years believing that my anger, my self-doubt, and my inability to trust others were personal failings. But therapy revealed a new narrative—one where my reactions were not weaknesses but signs of unresolved wounds. Dr. Darren explained how generational trauma, passed down from one generation to the next, can trap us in cycles of self-blame and guilt. This realization was freeing; it allowed me to view myself with more compassion and less judgment.

He also spoke of how self-blame becomes a tool of the mind's inner enemy, a force that keeps us locked in a cycle of suffering. By understanding this, I began to break free from that cycle. I learned to separate my worth from my past actions and from the pain I had endured.

Transformation: Integrating Insights and Moving Forward

The insights I gained in therapy were not just revelations to ponder—they were tools I could apply to my daily life. Slowly but surely, I started to integrate what I had learned into my thoughts and behaviors. The transformation was gradual but profound, marked by small, cumulative shifts.

One of the biggest transformations was learning to forgive—both myself and others. Forgiveness, I discovered, was not about excusing the wrongs done to me but about releasing the hold they had over my mind and heart. Therapy gave me the perspective to extend grace to those who had hurt me, and more importantly, to myself. I realized that true healing could not happen until I let go of the guilt and shame that had weighed me down for so long.

I also learned the importance of setting boundaries. Establishing emotional and mental boundaries became a way of protecting the progress I had made. It allowed me to honor my healing process, giving me the space to continue growing without falling back into old patterns.

Therapy, in many ways, was like peeling back the layers of an onion. With each session, I uncovered deeper truths about myself, truths that I had long buried beneath layers of coping mechanisms and defense strategies. As these layers fell away, I began to see myself more clearly and to reconnect with the parts of me that had been lost to pain.

In the end, therapy became a catalyst for profound growth and transformation. What began as a source of dread evolved into a powerful tool for understanding, healing, and personal evolution. The journey was neither linear nor easy; it required facing painful truths, confronting uncomfortable emotions, and questioning long-held beliefs. Yet, it also brought me a renewed sense of self, a deeper understanding of my past, and the tools to move forward with greater strength and clarity.

The battle of the mind is ongoing, but therapy taught me that it is a battle worth fighting. Through the process, I learned that healing is not about erasing the past, but about learning to live with it in a way that empowers rather than limits. Therapy, once seen as punishment, became my path to freedom.

Chapter 8: Generational Curses: Unraveling Family Patterns

Exodus 20:5-6 "You shall not bow down to them nor serve them. For I, the Lord your God, am a jealous God, visiting the iniquity of the fathers upon the children to the third and fourth generations of those who hate Me, but showing mercy to thousands, to those who love Me and keep My commandments."

Generational curses, those subtle, recurring patterns of pain and dysfunction that ripple through family lines, often lie hidden beneath the surface of our everyday lives. My path to healing and self-discovery was profoundly shaped by conversations with Grandma Rose, who became a key guide in uncovering these deep-seated patterns. This chapter explores the revelations gained from delving into my family's history, the concept of generational curses, and the critical importance of breaking these cycles for the sake of future generations.

Unearthing the Past:

My dialogues with Grandma Rose were eye-opening and transformative. These conversations opened a window into the struggles faced by the women in my family, particularly my mother and grandmother. As I sat with Grandma Rose, her stories of hardship and resilience offered a new lens through which to view the pain and challenges passed down through generations.

Grandma Rose referred to a "generational curse," a term she used to describe a recurring pattern of emotional and psychological struggles that affected the women in our family. These stories went beyond individual experiences, illustrating a continuum of trauma and strength that had shaped our family dynamics. Her narratives depicted how each generation grappled with their own battles, often without the resources or knowledge to break free from these cycles.

Understanding Generational Patterns: The Curse and Its Effects

Initially, grasping the concept of generational curses was challenging. It implied that the difficulties I faced were not isolated incidents but part of a larger, inherited pattern of dysfunction. This realization was both sobering and enlightening, as it helped me understand that my personal struggles were intertwined with the experiences of those before me.

For example, learning about my mother's emotional and psychological challenges shed light on how her experiences influenced her parenting. Her unresolved pain, though unintentional, had contributed to the difficulties I faced. This understanding allowed me to shift from a stance of blame and resentment to one of empathy and compassion.

Breaking the Cycle: The Commitment to Heal and Transform

Recognizing the generational patterns of pain and dysfunction brought a profound sense of responsibility. It became clear that breaking the cycle was not just about addressing my own issues but about transforming the legacy I would pass on to future generations. This commitment was both daunting and empowering.

To break the cycle, I needed to confront my own pain and work toward healing. This involved unlearning unhealthy patterns and redefining my understanding of love, relationships, and self-worth. It required a dedication to personal growth and a willingness to challenge the inherited beliefs and behaviors that had shaped my life.

During this process, I began releasing everything that had once weighed me down—the anger, the resentment, and the expectations I had placed on my mother. They all began to fade away as I embraced my identity in Christ. I was no longer bound by the past but was stepping into a new legacy, one built on faith, love, and strength. The generational curse that had cast its shadow over my family for so long was finally broken.

Creating a New Legacy: Practical Strategies for Change

Breaking the generational curse demanded practical strategies and tools. I began by setting clear boundaries and prioritizing self-care. These boundaries were not intended to isolate me but to protect my progress and ensure that I remained on a path of healing.

In addition to setting boundaries, I focused on building healthy relationships and cultivating a positive self-image. I made a conscious effort to model the behaviors and values I wanted to pass on to future generations. This included embracing forgiveness, practicing gratitude, and maintaining a hopeful outlook on life.

Seeking guidance from spiritual practices and therapy was also crucial. Regular prayer, meditation in God's word, and reflection helped me stay grounded and connected to a higher purpose. Therapy provided essential tools for managing emotions and addressing unresolved issues, contributing significantly to my overall well-being.

The Power of Understanding: Lessons for the Future

Understanding the generational courses within my family offered valuable insights into the broader context of my experiences. It illuminated the fact that my struggles were not unique but part of a larger family narrative. This understanding empowered me to take initiative-taking steps toward healing and transformation.

The lessons learned from exploring my family's history underscored the importance of breaking these cycles for future generations. By addressing and healing these patterns, I was not only improving my own life but also contributing to a more positive legacy for those who will follow.

Breaking generational curses is not a one-time effort but an ongoing journey of healing and transformation. It requires dedication, self-awareness, and a commitment to creating a new legacy of hope, resilience, and love. The process of understanding and addressing these patterns not only empowers individuals but also has the potential to positively impact future generations.

Chapter 9 - Forgiveness and Healing: A Journey to Self-Acceptance

Ephesians 4:32

"And be kind to one another, tenderhearted, forgiving one another, even as God in Christ forgave you."

Forgiveness is a journey deeply intertwined with healing and self-acceptance. For many, it is not merely an act but a profound process that requires navigating the complex landscape of guilt, pain, and grace. This chapter delves into the transformative journey of forgiveness, both for others and for oneself, and how it plays a crucial role in achieving self-acceptance.

The Struggle with Self-Forgiveness

Forgiving oneself can often be the most challenging aspect of healing. I found myself wrestling with deep-seated guilt and shame over past mistakes and decisions that, in hindsight, felt regretful. Despite knowing that God had forgiven me, I struggled to extend that same grace to myself. My mind was haunted by the belief that I should have known better, done better, and avoided the pitfalls that had caused me so much pain.

In conversations with my Bishop and through studying scriptures like Isaiah 55:7-9, I began to understand that God's forgiveness is a gift, not something earned through perfect behavior or self-punishment. These verses helped me grasp that God's ways and thoughts are far beyond mine, and His mercy is freely given, regardless of my past. This realization was crucial in beginning to forgive myself.

It was in therapy that the complexity of self-forgiveness became more evident. Dr. Darren's insights revealed that often, we internalize the pain caused by others and turn it inward, blaming ourselves for things beyond our control. The process of forgiving myself involved recognizing that the mistakes I had made were part of my journey, not a measure of my worth. It required acknowledging that my worth was defined by God's love and not by my failures.

The Journey of Forgiving Others

Forgiving others, especially those who have caused significant pain, is equally challenging. My journey toward forgiveness began with recognizing the pain inflicted by people like my father and others who had mistreated me. I had harbored deep-seated resentment and anger, feeling justified in my bitterness. However, these emotions only served to bind me to the past, preventing me from moving forward.

One of the most profound moments in this process was when I wrote letters to both my father and myself. In these letters, I confronted the pain and extended forgiveness. I wrote to my father, acknowledging that his inability to show love was not necessarily a reflection of me but a result of his own struggles and generational patterns. I came to understand that forgiveness was not about excusing his behavior but about releasing myself from the burden of anger and allowing healing to take its place.

Similarly, writing a letter to my younger self was a deeply emotional experience. It was a chance to communicate to the little girl who had been hurt and mistreated that it was not her fault. This exercise in self-compassion helped me separate my worth from the hurtful experiences and reassured me that I was deserving of love and grace.

Embracing Grace and Compassion

The core of forgiveness is grace, recognizing that we, too, need it. Embracing grace meant shifting my perspective from one of self-criticism and blame to one of understanding and compassion. I had to remind myself that just as God forgave me, I was called to forgive others and myself. This realization brought a meaningful change in how I viewed my past and myself.

Through this process, I began to see myself through the lens of grace rather than guilt. I learned that self-acceptance is not about being perfect but about being loved and valued despite imperfections. It meant accepting that I had made mistakes but that those mistakes did not define my entire existence. This shift in perspective allowed me to embrace my identity in Christ, a person worthy of love and deserving of peace.

Forgiveness also involved releasing the need for retribution and trusting that God's justice and mercy would prevail. As I reflected on the way Christ forgave those who wronged Him, even from the cross, it became evident that forgiveness was a path to freedom, not only for those who had wronged me but for myself.

The Path to Healing

Forgiveness was not a one-time act but a continual process of healing and growth. Each day presented an opportunity to practice grace, to let go of past grievances, and to reaffirm my identity in Christ. The journey toward self-acceptance was ongoing, involving regular reflection, prayer, and self-care.

Learning to view myself through a compassionate lens helped me build a more positive relationship with myself and others. It was a journey that required patience and perseverance but led to a deeper sense of peace and fulfillment.

This chapter illustrates the power of forgiveness and self-acceptance in the healing process. It underscores the importance of releasing guilt, extending grace, and embracing one is true worth. Through forgiveness, both of oneself and others, we find the path to healing and a renewed sense of self, grounded in love and compassion.

Chapter 10: Breaking the Chain: Embracing a New Legacy

2 Corinthians 5:17

"Therefore, if anyone is in Christ, he is a new creation; old things have passed away; behold, all things have become new."

Breaking free from the generational curse that had long influenced my family was both a challenge and a profound opportunity. Determined to create a new path for myself, I embarked on a journey of self-transformation, focusing on redefining my identity and establishing a healthier legacy. This chapter explores the steps I took to break the cycle of dysfunction and embrace a new, empowered way of living.

Embracing Personal Responsibility

The decision to break the chain of generational pain and dysfunction began with a conscious choice. I recognized that change required more than just a desire for a better future; it demanded a commitment to actively transform my life. This involved taking personal responsibility for my healing and growth, acknowledging that while I could not change the past, I had the power to shape my future.

I understood that breaking the generational curse was not solely about addressing my personal struggles but about creating a new legacy for future generations. This realization fueled my determination to embark on a path of self-transformation, where I would redefine what it meant to live a healthy, fulfilling life.

The Journey of Self-Discovery

A crucial part of my transformation was redefining my sense of self. This process involved unlearning old patterns and beliefs that had been ingrained in me through years of familial and subjective experiences. I began by exploring and questioning the core beliefs and behaviors that had shaped my identity.

One of the first steps in this journey was to engage in self-reflection. I spent time journaling, meditating, and seeking feedback from trusted individuals. These practices helped me gain clarity on who I truly was, beyond the limitations imposed by past traumas. I learned to distinguish between the person I was conditioned to be and the person I aspired to become.

Establishing Healthy Boundaries: Protecting My Progress

As I redefined my identity, establishing healthy boundaries became essential. These boundaries were not meant to isolate me but to safeguard my progress and ensure that my growth was not undermined by negative influences or old patterns.

I started by setting boundaries in my relationships, ensuring that I surrounded myself with people who supported my journey and respected my growth. This included distancing myself from toxic relationships and fostering connections with individuals who encouraged and uplifted me.

Additionally, I implemented boundaries in my personal life, prioritizing self-care and creating routines that supported my well-being. This involved setting aside time for activities that nourished my mind, body, and spirit, such as exercise, creative pursuits, and relaxation.

Building a New Legacy: Actions and Values

Creating a new legacy required more than just personal transformation; it involved actively building a life grounded in positive values and actions. I focused on establishing new habits and practices that reflected the healthier identity I was cultivating.

One of the key aspects of building this new legacy was redefining my understanding of love and relationships. I worked on cultivating relationships characterized by mutual respect, kindness, and open communication. This involved being intentional about how I interacted with others and ensuring that my relationships aligned with my values.

I also embraced new ways of thinking and behaving. I made a conscious effort to practice forgiveness, gratitude, and compassion. These values became central to my daily life, guiding my interactions with others and shaping my responses to challenges.

The Role of Faith: Trusting in Divine Guidance

Throughout this journey, my faith played a pivotal role in guiding and sustaining me. Trusting in God provided me with strength and hope as I navigated the complexities of transformation. I learned on my spiritual practices, such as prayer and meditation, to seek guidance and support.

Scriptures and spiritual teaching became sources of inspiration and reassurance. Verses like 2 Corinthians 4:16 reminded me that while the external challenges of life might persist, my inner renewal was a continuous process. This faith-based perspective helped me stay focused on the positive changes I was making and the new legacy I was creating.

Celebrating Milestones: Acknowledging Progress and Growth

As I continued this path of self-transformation, it was important to celebrate milestones and progress along the way. Recognizing and acknowledging the positive changes I was making helped reinforce my commitment to this new path.

I celebrated small victories, whether it was overcoming a long-standing fear, successfully setting, and maintaining boundaries, or cultivating a new, healthier relationship. These celebrations served as reminders of how far I had come and reinforced my belief in the possibility of a brighter future.

Moving Forward: Embracing a Future of Possibilities

Chapter 10 underscores the importance of breaking the generational chain and embracing a new legacy. By making a conscious decision to change, redefining my identity, establishing healthy boundaries, and building a life based on positive values, I embarked on a journey of self-transformation.

This chapter highlights that breaking the chain of dysfunction is an ongoing process that requires dedication and perseverance. Embracing a new legacy involves continuous growth, self-reflection, and a commitment to living a life that reflects the healthiest version of oneself. As I move forward, I carry with me the lessons learned from this journey and look toward a future filled with hope, purpose, and endless possibilities.

Chapter 11: Facing the Past: The Trial and Its Aftermath

Isaiah 43:18-19

"Do not remember the former things,
Nor consider the things of old.
Behold, I will do a new thing,
Now it shall spring forth;
Shall you not know it?
I will even make a road in the wilderness.
And rivers in the desert.

The final stages of my legal battle marked a profound chapter in my journey toward healing and justice. The emotional toll of this phase was significant, filled with complex feelings and challenging decisions. As I navigated the trial's conclusion and its aftermath, I encountered a range of emotions and faced the challenging task of reconciling my quest for justice with my need for personal peace and closure.

The Legal Battle: Preparing for the Trial

The anticipation of the trial was both daunting and exhausting. The legal process was a reminder of the public nature of my pain and the intricate web of judicial proceedings. Preparing for the trial involved a series of emotional and practical steps, from meeting with lawyers and reviewing evidence to recalling and recounting the traumatic events in detail.

I experienced a whirlwind of emotions as the trial approached—fear, anxiety, and a sense of vulnerability. The thought of reliving the trauma in a courtroom filled with strangers was overwhelming, but I was determined to seek justice. The trial became a battleground where I had to confront my past while striving to uphold my dignity and strength.

The Plea Deal: A Mixed Resolution

As the trial neared, the decision came that my attacker would plead guilty. This development was a significant moment in my journey, but it was met with mixed emotions. On one hand, the guilty plea meant that the legal process would conclude more swiftly, sparing me from the further trauma of a full trial. On the other hand, it left me grappling with unresolved feelings about the nature of justice and accountability.

The guilty plea felt like a validation of my pain and a form of justice, but it also brought with it a profound sense of ambivalence. I struggled with the idea that this resolution might not fully address the depth of my suffering or provide the closure I sought. The complexity of my emotions during this time was a testament to the multifaceted nature of healing and justice.

Emotional Toll: Navigating the Aftermath

The aftermath of the trial was a period of intense reflection and emotional processing. The legal resolution, while providing a sense of closure in one sense, did not erase the emotional scars left by the ordeal. I found myself grappling with a mix of relief, sadness, and lingering questions about the impact of the entire experience.

I sought solace in therapy and support from loved ones as I worked through the emotional toll of the trial's conclusion. The process of navigating my feelings and finding a sense of peace required patience and self-compassion. I recognized that healing from such a profound trauma was a journey with no clear endpoint, but rather a series of ongoing efforts to reconcile my past with my present.

Seeking Personal Peace: Balancing Justice and Healing

In the quest for justice, I realized that personal peace and closure were essential components of my healing journey. I worked to balance the desire for justice with the need to find inner peace and move forward.

This involved reflecting on my own emotional needs and making choices that supported my well-being.

I focused on practices that nurtured my healing, such as mindfulness, journaling, and engaging in activities that brought me joy and fulfillment. I also sought support groups and communities where I could share my experiences and connect with others who had faced similar challenges. These practices were integral in fostering a sense of peace and resilience as I continued to heal.

Reflecting on the Journey: Lessons Learned

The trial and its aftermath provided valuable lessons in resilience, strength, and self-compassion. I learned that seeking justice is not a linear process and that it often involves navigating complex emotions and decisions. The experience underscored the importance of addressing both the legal and emotional aspects of trauma.

I also recognized the significance of self-care and support during times of intense emotional strain. The journey through the trial highlighted the need to prioritize my mental and emotional well-being, even as I pursued justice. These lessons became integral to my ongoing healing process and shaped my approach to facing future challenges.

Moving Forward: Embracing a New Chapter

As I closed this chapter of my journey, I looked toward the future with a renewed sense of hope and determination. The legal battle and its aftermath were important milestones, but they were also part of a larger narrative of healing and growth. I carried forward the lessons learned, and the strength gained from this experience as I continued to build a life grounded in resilience and empowerment.

Chapter 11 captures the complexity of navigating the trial and its aftermath, revealing the intricate interplay between seeking justice and finding personal peace. It underscores the importance of acknowledging and addressing the emotional impact of such experiences while continuing to move forward with hope and strength.

Chapter 12: A New Dawn – Embracing a Future of Hope

Jeremiah 29:11 "For I know the thoughts that I think toward you, says the Lord, thoughts of peace and not of evil, to give you a future and a hope."

As the closing chapter of my journey begins to unfold, I find myself standing on the threshold of a new dawn, where healing and hope meet in perfect harmony. This chapter reflects not only on the profound transformation I have experienced but also on the ongoing effort to embrace a future filled with promise, peace, and possibility.

One song has become the anthem of my life, Yolanda Adams' "In the Midst of It All." This powerful hymn reminds me that even in my lowest moments, God was by my side, guiding me through every storm. The lyrics deeply resonate with my heart, capturing the essence of the battles I have fought and the divine grace that sustained me through them. As the song declares, "He never left me, He stood right by my side, and I wouldn't be here today if He hadn't sacrificed His life." These words have become my new declaration, a testament of faith that has carried me through the darkest nights and into the light of a new day.

In moments when life felt overwhelming, when the burdens seemed too heavy to bear, this song played in my spirit, reminding me that I was never truly alone. Even when I could not see it, God was there, carrying me when I could no longer stand, whispering words of life when I could not find the strength to pray. His presence was constant, unwavering, and filled me with a sense of hope even during uncertainty.

The Ongoing Journey of Healing

Healing is not a destination but a continuous journey, one that requires patience, reflection, and a commitment to growth. Looking back on the challenges I have faced, I realize that my journey is a testament to the strength I have developed, the resilience I have built, and the insight I have gained along the way. Each day, I continue to grow, learning more about myself, the world around me, and the beauty of the process.

The practices that support my healing—therapy, mindfulness, self-care—are not just habits. They are the foundations of my well-being. Engaging in these practices helps me nurture my soul, maintain balance, and stay connected to the progress I have made. Healing is not linear, and there are days when the road feels long and difficult, but with each step, I remind myself that growth is happening, even if it is not immediately visible.

Rebuilding Relationships: A Path to Connection

One of the most challenging, yet rewarding, aspects of my journey has been the effort to rebuild my relationship with my father. Our relationship has been complicated, marked by misunderstandings, distance, and pain. But through it all, I have approached our reconnection with hope and openness, willing to confront the past to build something new.

This process has required patience, vulnerability, and a lot of difficult conversations. We have set boundaries, addressed old grievances, and slowly started to rebuild trust. Reconnecting is not easy; it is a journey. But the small steps we have taken have brought us closer to a future that holds the promise of a stronger, healthier relationship. I have learned that healing relationships takes time, effort, and a willingness to engage with the messiness of human connection. It is not always perfect, but it is worth it.

Setting Boundaries: Protecting My Progress

As I continue to heal, one of the most important lessons I have learned is the necessity of setting boundaries. Boundaries are essential for protecting my emotional and mental well-being, ensuring that I stay grounded in the growth I have achieved. They are not walls meant to keep others out, but guidelines that allow me to thrive and continue my journey of healing.

I have come to understand the importance of clearly communicating my needs and protecting my space. Boundaries have given me the clarity and confidence to navigate relationships with intention. By setting and honoring these boundaries, I create an environment where I can continue to heal and grow, safeguarding the progress I have made.

Embracing the Future of Hope

Looking forward, I am filled with hope and optimism. The past has undoubtedly shaped me, but it is the future that excites me—the possibilities of who I will become and the life I will build. I step into this new chapter with a sense of renewal, knowing that the lessons I have learned have equipped me with the strength, resilience, and faith to face whatever comes next.

Hope has become my guiding force. It is the light that drives me forward, even in moments of uncertainty. It inspires me to pursue a future that reflects my values, dreams, and the growth that has emerged from my journey of healing. The road ahead may not always be easy, but it is filled with opportunity, promise, and the chance to live authentically and fully.

The Dawn of a New Chapter

As I close this chapter of my life, I want to leave you with this truth: pain may have shaped me, but it was trauma that healed me. The deep wounds of my past pushed me to confront the darkness, to seek out the light, and to discover strength in my faith that I never knew existed.

I am no longer the person I once was. I am stronger, wiser, and more compassionate. I have learned the power of forgiveness, the necessity of letting go, and the beauty of trusting in God's plan for my life. Most importantly, I have realized that my story is not defined by the pain I endured, but by the healing and growth that has come from it.

The song of my life has changed. It is no longer one of sorrow or defeat, but of victory and grace. Just as Yolanda Adams sings, I can confidently declare that God has been with me through it all guiding, protecting, and loving me through every trial. For that, I am eternally grateful. This is my new song, one of hope, faith, and unwavering strength.

This chapter is not just the conclusion of one journey but the beginning of another, one filled with possibility and hope. The past has played its role, but it is the future that will define who I become. With each new day, I step forward with courage, strength, and the unshakable belief in the power of resilience.

A Message of Encouragement

To those who are also on their journey of healing, I offer this message of hope: the path may be winding, but it is full of opportunities for growth, transformation, and renewal. Embrace the process with patience, kindness, and compassion for yourself. Remember that your past does not dictate your future.

Each step forward, no matter how small, is a victory. Surround yourself with love and support, take care of yourself, and keep moving toward the life you envision. Your journey, like mine, is a testament to the resilience and hope that resides within all of us.

This chapter, "A New Dawn," captures the essence of embracing a hopeful future while honoring the ongoing nature of healing. It highlights the importance of setting boundaries, rebuilding relationships, and stepping into the future with optimism, strength, and grace.

Epilogue

The sun set over the horizon, casting a golden hue over the world as if bidding a final farewell to the remnants of the day. The journey had been long and arduous, filled with trials, triumphs, and countless moments of doubt. Yet, as the last rays of light kissed the earth, it was clear that every step had been worth it. The bonds forged, the lessons learned, and the growth experienced were treasures that would endure beyond the passage of time.

In the quiet aftermath, the characters found themselves standing at the threshold of new beginnings. They were no longer the same individuals who had embarked on this journey, but rather, they were stronger, wiser, and more resilient. The challenges they faced had not only evaluated their limits but had also revealed the depths of their courage and the strength of their spirit.

The story, however, does not end here. It lives on in the hearts and minds of those who have traveled alongside the characters. It is a testament to the enduring power of hope, the unyielding strength of love, and the transformative potential of perseverance. As the final chapter closes, a new one begins, filled with endless possibilities and the promise of a brighter tomorrow.

Letter to the Reader

Dear Reader,

Thank you for joining me on this remarkable journey. As we reach the end of this story, I find myself filled with a profound sense of gratitude for the time we have shared and the experiences we have encountered together.

Writing this book has been a labor of love, a process that has allowed me to explore the depths of human emotion and the resilience of the human spirit. It has been my hope that within these pages, you have found moments of reflection, inspiration, and even a sense of connection to the characters and their struggles.

Stories have a unique power to transcend time and space, to bridge the gap between different lives and experiences. They remind us that we are not alone, that our fears, dreams, and aspirations are shared by others, and that we are all part of a larger tapestry of humanity.

As you close this book, I encourage you to carry its lessons with you. Remember the strength you possess, the importance of love and kindness, and the beauty of perseverance. Let the story be a beacon of hope in times of darkness and a source of comfort in moments of uncertainty.

I am deeply grateful for your readership and for the opportunity to share this story with you. Your support means more to me than words can express, and it is my sincere hope that this book has touched your heart in some small way.

With heartfelt appreciation,
Michaelia Nobles

About the Author

Michaelia Nobles is a talented creator, author, and communicator with a passion for storytelling that inspires and uplifts. She is set to make her literary debut with the highly anticipated book Pain Raised Me but Trauma Healed Me, releasing on November 15th. This work reflects her personal journey through life's challenges, emphasizing the resilience and strength found in overcoming adversity.

Currently pursuing a bachelor's degree in media and communications, a field that perfectly aligns with her passion for storytelling and her desire to make a meaningful impact. Her academic journey has provided her with a strong foundation in media, writing, and communication, equipping her with the skills to navigate the ever-evolving landscape of the media industry.

In addition to her writing, Michaelia is also the host of the Just Keep It Real Podcast, where she engages in candid conversations about life, faith, and the importance of reality. Her ability to connect with others and share real-life stories has gained her a growing audience who appreciate her genuine approach and insightful perspectives.

Michaelia's talents extend beyond writing and podcasting; she is also an experienced public speaker, known for her compelling and significant delivery. Her speaking engagements often center around themes of personal growth, faith, and the power of perseverance. She is deeply committed to sharing her story and helping others find their voice in the process.With a heart for service and a drive to make a difference, Michaelia Nobles is on a mission to inspire others through her work, her words, and her unwavering commitment to keeping it real. Whether through her writing, podcasting, or public speaking, she aims to empower others to face their challenges head-on